187208

PowerKids Readers:

The Bilingual Library of the United States of America™

ALASKA

JOSÉ MARÍA OBREGÓN

TRADUCCIÓN AL ESPAÑOL: MARÍA CRISTINA BRUSCA

The Rosen Publishing Group's
PowerKids Press™ & **Editorial Buenas Letras**™
New York

Published in 2005 by The Rosen Publishing Group, Inc.
29 East 21st Street, New York, NY 10010

First Edition

Photo Credits: Cover, p. 30 (State Nickname) © Dale Jorgensen/SuperStock, Inc.; p. 5 © Joe Sohm/The Image Works; p. 7 © 2002 Geoatlas; pp. 9, 11 (Caribou), 31 (Highest) © Paul A. Souders/Corbis; p. 11 (Bear) © Charles Mauzy/Corbis; pp. 11 (Wolf), 19, 31 (Sled Dog Race) © Kennan Ward/Corbis; pp. 11 (Seal), 30 (Willow Ptarmigan) © Steve Kaufman/Corbis; pp. 13, 21 © Galen Rowell/Corbis; p. 15 Alaska State Library/01-2302; p. 17 © Corbis; p. 23 © Michael DeYoung/Corbis; pp. 25, 30 (Capital) © Joseph Sohm; ChromoSohm Inc./Corbis; pp. 26, 30 (Sitka Spruce) © Tom Bean/Corbis; p. 30 (Forget-me-not) © James L. Amos/Corbis; p. 30 (Jade) © Maurice Nimmo; Frank Lane Picture Agency/Corbis; p. 31 (Juneau) Alaska State Library/ASL-P20-12; p. 31 (Peratrovich) Alaska State Library; p. 31 (Rock) Alaska State Library/UAF-1992-202-12; p. 31 (Egan) © Bettmann/Corbis; p. 31 (Moe) © Orban/Corbis Sygma; p. 31 (Gomez) © Ciniglio Lorenzo/Corbis Sygma

Library of Congress Cataloging-in-Publication Data

Obregón, José María, 1963–
    Alaska / José María Obregón; traducción al español, María Cristina Brusca.— 1st ed.
        p. cm. — (The bilingual library of the United States of America)
    Includes bibliographical references and index.
    ISBN 1-4042-3066-1 (library binding)
    1. Alaska—Juvenile literature. I. Title. II. Series.

F904.3.O27 2005/
979.8–dc22

                                                    2004029732

Manufactured in the United States of America

Due to the changing nature of Internet links, Editorial Buenas Letras has developed an online list of Web sites related to the subject of this book. This site is updated regularly. Please use this link to access the list:

http://www.buenasletraslinks.com/ls/alaska

Contents

Contenido

Welcome to Alaska

These are the flag and seal of Alaska. A 13-year-old boy named Benny Benson drew the flag in 1926.

Bienvenidos a Alaska

Éstos son la bandera y el escudo de Alaska. Un chico de 13 años llamado Benny Benson, dibujó la bandera en 1926.

The Alaska Flag and the State Seal

La bandera y el escudo de Alaska

Alaska Geography

Alaska is in the far north. Alaska borders the country of Canada and is very close to Russia! Alaska is not connected to the rest of the United States.

Geografía de Alaska

Alaska está en el extremo norte. Alaska linda con Canadá. ¡También está muy cerca de Rusia! El territorio de Alaska no está conectado al resto de los Estados Unidos.

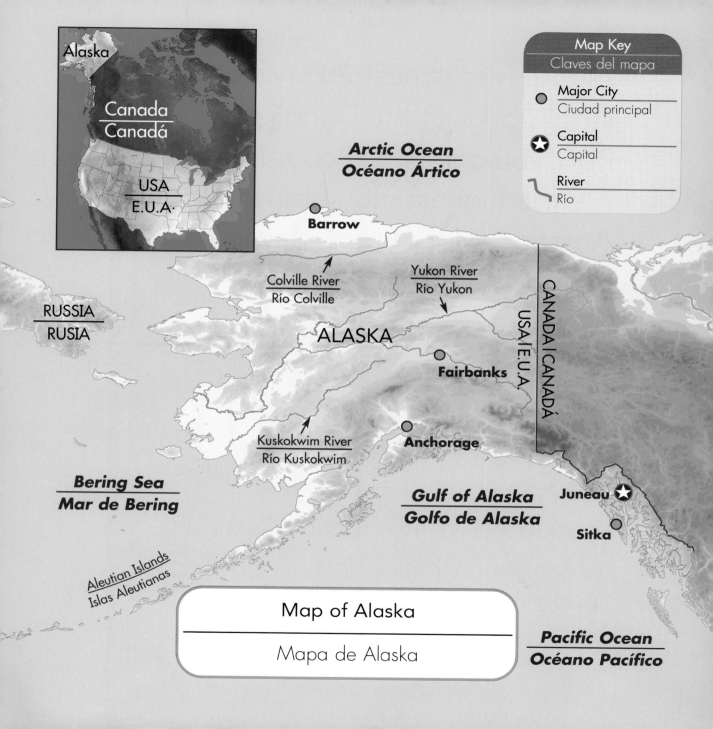

Alaska

Canada
Canadá

USA
E.U.A.

Arctic Ocean
Océano Ártico

● Barrow

Colville River
Río Colville

Yukon River
Río Yukon

RUSSIA
RUSIA

ALASKA

CANADA | CANADÁ

USA | E.U.A.

● Fairbanks

Kuskokwim River
Río Kuskokwim

● Anchorage

Bering Sea
Mar de Bering

Gulf of Alaska
Golfo de Alaska

Juneau ★

Sitka ●

Aleutian Islands
Islas Aleutianas

Map of Alaska

Mapa de Alaska

Pacific Ocean
Océano Pacífico

Alaska has almost 200 national and state parks. In the Denali National Park you can find Mount McKinley. It is the highest mountain in North America. Mount McKinley is 20,320 feet (6,193 m) high!

Alaska tiene casi 200 parques nacionales y estatales. En el Parque Nacional Denali puedes encontrar el Monte McKinley. Esta montaña es la más alta de Norteamérica. ¡El Monte McKinley tiene 20,320 pies (6,193m) de altura!

A View of Mount McKinley

Vista del Monte McKinley

Alaska is home to many wild animals. Caribou, grizzly bears, gray wolves, and fur seals live in Alaska.

Alaska es el hogar de muchos animales salvajes. En Alaska viven caribús, osos pardos, lobos grises y focas.

Alaska History

Alaskan natives have been living on this land for more than 10,000 years. Alaskan native groups include the Aleuts, the Yupik, the Inupiat Eskimos, the Athabascans, the Tlingits, the Tsimshian, and the Haida.

Historia de Alaska

Los nativos de Alaska han vivido en esta tierra por más de 10,000 años. Los grupos nativos de Alaska incluyen a los aleut, yupik, inupiat eskimos, athabascan, tlingit, tsimshian y haida.

Alaska Natives Dressed in Their Finest Winter Furs

Nativos de Alaska vestidos en elegantes abrigos de piel

The explorer Vitus Bering was the first European to visit Alaska, in 1741. He proved that North America and the Russian region of Siberia were separated by water.

Vitus Bering fue el primer explorador europeo en visitar Alaska, en 1741. Bering comprobó que Norteamérica y la región rusa de Siberia estaban separadas por agua.

Explorer Vitus Bering

El explorador Vitus Bering

After the Bering trips Alaska became Russian land. In 1867, the United States bought Alaska from the Russians. William H. Seward signed the purchase for the American government on March 30, 1867.

Después de los viajes de Bering, Alaska pasó a ser parte de Rusia. En 1867, Estados Unidos compró Alaska a los rusos. William H. Seward firmó la compra en nombre del gobierno estadounidense el 30 de marzo de 1867.

William H. Seward

Living in Alaska

Alaskans have used dogs for transportation for many years. Today sled dog races are a very popular sport in Alaska. Sled dog races are part of many winter festivals.

La vida en Alaska

Durante años, los alasqueños han usado perros para transportarse. Hoy día, las carreras de trineos son un deporte muy popular en Alaska y son parte de muchos festivales invernales.

Sled Dog Race in Anchorage, Alaska

Carrera de trineos en Anchorage, Alaska

Summers in Alaska are short, but the Sun shines 20 hours per day. In the city of Barrow the Sun shines 24 hours per day for 12 weeks!

Los veranos en Alaska son cortos pero el sol alumbra 20 horas por día. ¡En la ciudad de Barrow el sol brilla 24 horas por día durante 12 semanas!

A View of the City of Barrow, Alaska

Vista de la ciudad de Barrow en Alaska

Alaska Today

Alaskans are proud of their traditions and their great land. They work very hard to keep the wildlife and the beauty of their land.

Alaska, hoy

Los alasqueños están muy orgullosos de sus tradiciones y de su magnífica tierra. Ellos trabajan duramente para mantener la vida silvestre y la belleza de su tierra.

A Caribou in the Alaskan Tundra

Un caribú en la tundra de Alaska

In size Alaska is the biggest state in our country. Anchorage, Fairbanks, Sitka, and Juneau are important cities in Alaska. Juneau is the capital of the state.

Por su tamaño, Alaska es el estado más grande de nuestro país. Anchorage, Fairbanks, Sitka y Juneau son ciudades importantes de Alaska. Juneau es la capital del estado.

The Capitol Building in Juneau

Capitolio en la ciudad de Juneau

Activity:
Let's Draw Alaska's State Tree
The Sitka spruce became Alaska's official state tree in 1962.

Actividad:
Dibujemos el árbol del estado de Alaska
El abeto Sitka es el árbol oficial del estado de Alaska desde 1962.

1

Draw a tall, thin triangle. This is the trunk.

Dibuja un triángulo delgado y alto. Éste es el tronco.

2

Draw lines on either side of the trunk. Notice that the branches are longer as you go down the trunk.

Dibuja líneas a ambos lados del tronco. A medida que bajas por el tronco las ramas son más largas.

26

3

Turn your pencil on its side and shade from side to side on top of the trunk.
Shade up and down along the branches with short, gentle strokes.

Pon tu lápiz de costado y sombrea de un lado al otro por encima del tronco.
Sombrea las ramas con trazos verticales cortos y suaves.

4

To draw the needles, darken the shaded areas. Finish shading the trunk by turning your pencil on its side again.

Para dibujar las agujas oscurece las zonas sombreadas. Termina de sombrear el tronco, nuevamente con el lápiz de costado.

Timeline

1741	Vitus Bering expedition founds Alaska on July 15.
1778	Captain James Cook charts Alaska's coastline.
1867	U.S. purchases Alaska from Russia.
1896	Gold is discovered on Klondike River.
1942	Japan bombs Dutch Harbor.
1959	Alaska becomes the forty-ninth state of the Union.
1964	Good Friday earthquake kills 131 people.
1989	The *Exxon Valdez*, an oil supertanker, produces the worst oil spill in U.S. history.

Cronología

1741	La expedición de Vitus Bering descubre Alaska, el 15 de julio.
1778	El capitán James Cook dibuja el mapa de la costa de Alaska.
1867	E.U.A. compra Alaska a Rusia.
1896	Se descubre oro en el Río Klondike.
1942	Japón bombardea Dutch Harbor.
1959	Alaska se convierte en el estado de la Unión número cuarenta y nueve.
1964	El terremoto del Viernes Santo mata 131 personas.
1989	El buque petrolero Exxon Valdez produce el peor derrame de petróleo en la historia de E.U.A.

Alaska Events

January
Russian Christmas
Winter Sunrise in Barrow

March
Iditarod Trail Sled Dog Race

April
Alaska Folk Festival in Juneau

May
The Midnight Sun in Barrow

June
Summer Solstice Celebrations

July
World Eskimo-Indian Olympics
in Fairbanks

August–September
State Fair in Palmer

October
Alaska Day Celebrations in Sitka

December
Athabascan Fiddling Festival
in Fairbanks

Eventos en Alaska

Enero
Navidad rusa
Amanecer invernal en Barrow

Marzo
Carrera de trineos Iditarod Trail

Abril
Festival folclórico de Alaska, en Juneau

Mayo
Sol de medianoche, en Barrow

Junio
Celebraciones del solsticio de verano

Julio
Olimpíadas mundiales esquimo-indias,
en Fairbanks

Agosto-septiembre
Feria del estado, en Palmer

Octubre
Celebraciones del Día de Alaska, en Sitka

Diciembre
Festival atabascano de violín,
en Fairbanks

Alaska Facts/Datos sobre Alaska

Population
626,932

Población
626,932

Capital
Juneau

Capital
Juneau

State Motto
North to the Future

Lema del estado
Hacia el Norte, hacia el futuro

State Flower
Forget-me-not

Flor del estado
Nomeolvides

State Bird
Willow ptarmigan

Ave del estado
Lagópodo escandinavo

State Nickname
The Last Frontier

Mote del estado
La Última Frontera

State Tree
Sitka spruce

Árbol del estado
Abeto Sitka

State Song
"Alaska's Flag"

Canción del estado
"La bandera de Alaska"

State Gemstone
Jade

Piedra preciosa
Jade

Famous Alaskans/Alasqueños famosos

Joseph Juneau
(1826–1890)

Gold prospector
Buscador de oro

Elizabeth Peratrovich
(1911–1958)

Civil rights activist
Activista de derechos civiles

Howard Rock
(1911–   )

Eskimo activist
Activista esquimal

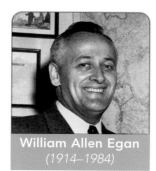

William Allen Egan
(1914–1984)

Alaska's first governor
Primer gobernador de Alaska

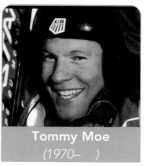

Tommy Moe
(1970–   )

Olympic medalist
Campeón olímpico

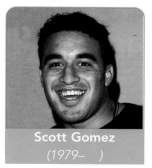

Scott Gomez
(1979–   )

Hockey player
Jugador de Hockey

Words to Know/Palabras que debes saber

border
frontera

highest
el más alto

territory
territorio

sled dog race
carreras de trineos

31

Here are more books to read about Alaska:
Otros libros que puedes leer sobre Alaska:

In English/En inglés:

Alaska,
America the Beautiful Series
By Walsh Shepherd, Donna
Children's Press, 1999

Alaska
Hello U.S.A.
By Johnston, Joyce
Lerner Publications, 1994

Words in English: 290

Palabras en español: 293

Index

Índice